God Above Sky

NEHEMY N. KIHARA

ISBN:1540449408
ISBN-13:978-1540449405

DEDICATION

Dedicated to my late 1st sister-in-law
Mrs.Margaret Wanjiru Githyaka-Gathogo, late wife of my
elder brother Samwel Gathogo Kihara(Big Sam);
Kalalu Community Elder (Laikipia County)
who while fighting cancer assured us that
her eyes were set on the God above All.
To all modern, native and indigenous Peoples on
Mother Earth and under the Sun and Moon;
Who by Words (Beliefs)and Deeds(Rituals)
Revere and Worship, the Timeless and Spaceless,
Creator Above Skyways.

CONTENTS

ACKNOWLEDGMENTS

Acknowledgments go to all my teachers;
My parents who taught me human values.
My village neighbors who taught me social ethics and
school teachers who taught me how to read, write and count
Thanks go to all my readers, and students, in Sunday school,
High school and University, for always teaching me something new.
Thanks go to many others, including religious believers,
who always remind me of the presence of the
Creator Above Skyways in our everyday interactions,
In times of the joy of birth, life of feast, rest ,work
and uncertainty of death and dying.

1 INTRODUCTION

My immediate task is to analyze the Religious Situation of Modern Africa. To do this adequately requires a series of books. But in this book I will attempt to examine only the unique features concerned with the background of Africa's cultural heritage.

The religious situation and the challenges which the African religious communities must face, in common with the whole of the human civilization in an increasingly industrial and technological age.

The unique aspect of the religious situation in Africa consists in the degree of the diversity and pluralism of our cultural and religious life.

Africa is a continent composed of more than 50 nation-states, and over 1,000 ethnic and linguistic groups, on the religious side many Christian sects and churches (Protestants as well as Catholics). There are Muslims and also deep in the souls of the African people the tendency towards the indigenous religion (its beliefs and rituals).

The other major world religions - the Hindu, Buddhist, Zoroastrian, Confucians, and Sikhs - all find a place in Africa, too.

2. AFRICAN RELIGIOUS HERITAGE

Every activity was organized on this belief on the supernatural and almighty Being - the Supplier and Distributor of all ultimate needs of life. The society was based on this belief. There was no division of the secular and the sacred - the sacred was experienced in the context of the secular. Religious behavior was experienced in the context of the community life.

In this sense we can undoubtedly say that Africa has a religious tradition or a traditional religion. Any African who can today advocate atheism is nothing short of a first degree hypocrite, advocating a deep meaninglessness foreign to the African personality and cultural heritage.

It was unfortunate and a mere sign of ignorance that the early Europeans overlooked this rich religious heritage in their process of "missionization". And a mere show of pride and cultural chauvinism that they continually insulted (some still do so) the Africans by calling them animists, pagans, and atheists.

Today the majority of Africans, far from being unbelievers, are traditional religionists, especially the Western, Central, Eastern and Southern Africa.

These believe in the "Creator Above the Skyways" (not native gods, who are a creation of Western interpretations of Africans' religious behavior). Their beliefs and practices are not institutionalized, but are common rituals that respect that advocate for human dignity, justice and the spiritual reality in everyday social life.

In North Africa, also there were and still are indigenous religionists; Islam is the established religion. It is in this part of the continent that Christianity entered Africa during the early century A.D. Immediately after its birth in the Middle East - Palestine.

According to traditions, St. Mark, the Evangelist began the Church in Egypt at the dawn of the Christian Era. Then Christianity spread into Ethiopia on the Eastern Africa coast.

Here the Coptic Church became the State Church, and with the nation maintaining its authenticity from foreign powers for a long time, Christianity existed here up to date.

Note that in the Book of Acts an Ethiopian eunuch, a body guard to the ruling Queen, was reading the book of Isaiah (the Scriptures) when Philip, the evangelist, Christianized him through faith and baptism (Acts 8:35).

With all historical evidence authority we can say that Christianity reached and was established in Africa before it spread into Europe. But for reasons such as Islamization and migrations that will be given on the next statement.

The present-day churches in Africa were as a result of the missionary movement of the 16th century onwards - starting with the mission work of the Roman Catholics in Western Africa (Congo and Angola). This may be considered the first enterprise of modern Christian missions.

3 THE EARLY CHURCH AND AFRICANS

The Early Church (whose story the Book of Acts records) had a branch in Africa (North). This means that Christianity apart from the African traditional religion, was the first amongst other religions to enter the continent of the Africoid (nine of the early Church Leaders were Africans).

Somehow, many Africanist scholars such as Oshitelu (2002) recognize them as Africans, while others tend to call them Roman or Latin, despite their birth in such well known African countries of Algeria or Tunisia.

These leaders were; <u>Athanasius</u> (296-373) <u>Augustine</u> (354-430), <u>Cyprian</u> (200-258); <u>Clement</u> (150-215), <u>Cyril</u> (375-444), <u>Dionysius</u> (200-263), <u>Didymus</u> (313-398), <u>Origen</u> (185-254), <u>Tertullian</u> (155-220).

However, in the 7th century - Islam religion came next with the Arabs from Arabia who came in 640 A.D. to Egypt and by 681 A.D. had taken it over as their own.

In 8th century, the Christian church in Africa (northern) whose converts were poorly taught, later overrun, swept and doomed to extinction. Only in Northern Sudan, a form of it survived for some time until the 17th century.

4 ISLAM IN AFRICA

<u>The Muslim Religion</u> with this conquest Islam spread and became powerful enough to create the modern day - Islamic states in Northern, Western, and Central Africa. Amongst these are Egypt, Libya, Tunisia, Algeria, Morocco, Sahara, Mauritania, Sudan, and Somalia (in Eastern Africa).

Islamic leadership includes some other countries in Western and Central Africa. Interestingly enough, most African countries above the equator who are not Islamic, have in their northern portion some form of Islam.

<u>State Religion: Islam in North Africa</u>

<u>Islam as the state religion</u> in North Africa dominates the (Sharia) legal systems of the nations concerned. However, today, there are trends towards reformation and change in the states where scientific socialism or Marxist-Leninist ideology is adopted (Libya, Somalia, and Algeria are examples).

Furthermore, Islam itself has a number of sects as practiced in the African scene. Leading amongst these the Ahmadiya an offshoot of Orthodox Sunni Moslems.

The Appeal of Islam to Africans

The Muslim religion today is progressing and more aggressive as ever, this time the sword being used in other ways than just jihad [holy war].

Moreover, unlike Mission Christianity, Islam appeals to Africans. In other words, Islam features some attractiveness in that unlike Christianity it imposes no standard of morality.

In the past this was possible because it was spread by Africans in the villages, who were a part of the community. Hardcore and extremist jihadists, committed to spreading terrorism and intimidation, are making it hard for Muslims in Africa, who live peacefully with all others .

The Arabs by becoming Egyptians or North Africans were a part of the community , with no racial or cultural barriers, like the 'white' pinkish colored European missionaries who were seen as strangers, and worse as intruders.

Today, the independent Muslim countries or Islamic leadership, with anti-western sentiment reinforces that religion and its acceptance by Africans.

The behavior of some Christian missionaries, strengthened the notion that Christianity is a foreign religion ('white' man's religion). This they did by their "religiously immoral" behavior which was unbecoming and questionable by both African and even western standards.

The Preference and Growth of Islam

As a matter of fact the current trend of Islamization is a great concern in Christian circles and Churches.

According to Encyclopedia Britannica Book of the Year, 1977, in Africa, there were 101,889,500 Moslems in comparison with 98,336,000 Christians (Protestants, Eastern Orthodox, and Catholics).

Since the Protestant figures include full members rather than all baptized person, the statistical accuracy is not absolute, but at least we can see that a difference which prefers Moslems can be clearly seen.

5 CHRISTIANITY IN AFRICA

The Setback of Christianity

As stated elsewhere, the Christian religion in Africa faced a great set back. In the beginning it suffered a setback in the extinction of the early Church.

During the period of missionary movements, the Sahara Desert blocked any possible travelling northward by the missionaries, so they concentrated on the Western, Central, Eastern, and Southern parts of the Continent.

Altogether for those who could come directly to northern Africa - there was a legal prohibition of evangelization or Christian missionization in almost all Islamic states - Tunisia, Morocco, and Libya being in the forefront. The other set back was centered on the missionaries themselves and their activities.

These like any other human beings, happened to belong to a particular race - the Caucasoid. They were a part and parcel of European Civilization, and loyal to their home governments, to whom they paid their allegiance.

Christianization and Colonialization

Their coming to Africa was at the same time the coming of European explorers and traders, worst of all the slave traders and colonialists (Colonizers).

Positive Side of Missionization

Thanks to God, their positive contribution/advanced literacy (education), medicine (hospitals) and built schools and churches in the name of the Gospel the Good News of God's eternal love to save humanity in Jesus Christ. Their zeal and devotion changed the face and destiny of the continent.

African Indigenous Missionaries

The history of Christianity in Africa is filled with accounts of these servants of God, who underwent severe physical and even psychological hardships so as to make the "Unknown God" spiritually revealed in Jesus Christ, to be known by the African whose worshipping behavior was a prepared ground.

Together with these there are accounts of African missionaries:

-Prince Kaboo, better known as Sammy Morris of Liberia, who died in U.S.A. probably as the first African missionary to America.

-Thomas Burch Freeman also Western Africa.

-Dr. J.E. Kwegir Aggrey of Ghana (formerly Gold Coast)

-Bishop Samuel Adjir Crowther of Nigeria and the Eastern African

-Apolo Kivebulaya of Uganda - the missionary to the pygmies of the Congo.

Euro-American Missionaries

These Africans and their counterpart European and American missionaries such as Robert Moffat, Dr. David Livingstone, Henry Stanley, Andrew Murray, Peter Cameron Scott - and many others that followed or accompanied them are a testimony of a people who gave their lives for others.

Such men and women are found in almost all corners of the western world, even here in Atlanta.

Negative side of Missionization

However, there is the other side of the coin that needs to be examined, too, if the picture will be complete. This is what I call the negative contribution.

As we said elsewhere, the missionaries were human beings - with limitations present to all of us. Yet some of them failed to recognize that factor (according to is known thus far, the larger number belonged to this category).

These being motivated by the European desire to conquer and rule and the domino motto of divide and rule, the confused the call of the Gospel with their racial (white) package, under whose flag they came to the continent.

Therefore, the Gospel of truth, love, and justice for all (oids) types of people Africoid, Caucasoid, and Mongoloid races of humanity, was confused with the so-called white (supposedly standing for purity).

Civilization and imperialism or superiority of the pinkish colored Caucasoid race over the Africoid and Mongoloid whose fate was only that of servitude and subjection in slavery.

6 MISSIONARY COLLABORATION WITH COLONIALISM

Missionary Collaboration with Colonialism

These collaborated with the colonialists - their Caucasoid brothers who at this time were not only ruling the Negroid peoples inhabiting Africa (but also the Mongoloid peoples of Asia and Latin America - all parts of the present day deprived Third World).

The best documentation of what was going on is the Southern Africa - where the Dutch Reformed Church - and others, all products of missionary activity is a part of the oppressive and racist apartheid system and policy dominated by white bigots (pardon my use of strong words if it hurts).

Central amongst the negative contributions of the missionary movements is not only the oppressive colonialism and slavery but also racism .

Prejudice or the claim of superiority of one's race over against other's which ones seeks to subdue, as opposed to the recognition of racial differences and their similarities in the unified human race of mankind ; Homo Sapiens (the so called collective races of Black, Yellow, Whites, and the shades in between them).

The Africans did not create racism , the Europeans or 'whites' made it and propagated it as the vanguard of their so called Christian civilization.

Education which was supposed to be a positive contribution when used as a means of domestication of the Africans, so as to be subject to the colonial powers, became a negative contribution. Today the question is centered on the creation of elite class, amongst them those who are ruling today.

Following the old game of colonialism - exploitation and oppression, these as puppets of the same colonial powers even after independence continue to suppress their fellow (blacks) Africans.

Condemnation of African Culture

The African culture - was condemned by the missionaries (negative contribution). A people cannot exist without a culture, therefore through domestication the Western culture filled the emptied Africans.

Any person aware of the African situation and mostly the personality, knows that one lives in a dilemma. For example as an African , the traditional culture compels me to jump in joy while singing, but since that is dancing, and the missionaries condemned dancing as incompatible with the Christian life ; then as a Christian, I cannot dance , as a result my singing becomes dull and not authentic.

Furthermore the Westerners introduced dancing in the nightclubs, the place where people enjoy it without restrictions. The dilemma now is; if I dance I am judged as much as anyone who is a nightclub frequenter, to be Christian is therefore to be contented with dullness.

That is just one example amongst many others, created by the dichotomy between the westernized sacred and the secular. We find it hard to experience the sacred in the context of the secular as an African people.

7 AFRICAN CHRISTIANS AND MISSION CHURCH

African Christians and Church

The Christian Church in Africa, therefore is in a dilemma that cannot be solved as one would do to a problem. But a situation which have to be lived with.

Christianity has become a reality in Africa .Christ is God incarnate in the human which includes Africa. Therefore He is a Reality in Africa not a foreigner.

However, the African Christians are seeking to understand GOD and interpret their relationship with Him in the context of their everyday life, that is their social and cultural context.

Christ is the only one who can give an ultimate meaning to their existence, but even Christ is experienced in the context of culture. The past and the present form of existence, the struggle of human beings with themselves and their environment to survival. In this process they create culture as a meaning giving factor.

Recently the African Churches have had two alternatives to this dilemma. To indigenous their Church make it address itself to the needs of the people in the context of their life.

The other is to do nothing and continue being condemned by their independent government, as western and non-progressive institutions. The indigenization has been found to be more compatible with the African situation and peoples cultural context.

Two patterns have emerged in the implementation of this:

1. Some churches - in the form of sects - have broken away as independent churches free from missionary influence and control. These interpret the Christian teachings in the light of the African traditional religion.

2. The Missionary produced Churches or the historic churches have started by Africanizing their leadership, without breaking their missionary (white) ties while others have called for a moratorium on Western Missionary personnel and support for a period of 5 years.

3. This period will help them to develop their own identity, as African Christian Churches and their selfhood, as no longer young children in need of paternalism and supervision, but as a responsible Body of Christ in the African context capable of training and educating her members.

Cultural renewal and revolution

Increasingly, the Government pressures have forced the Church to take a stand on the question of Cultural Renewal and Revolution, this accelerates the issues of the direction Christianity has to go, if it will make sense and give meaning to the African people.

The situation has resulted into persecution and hostile relationship with the State in several places such as, Chad and Congo DRC then known as Zaire ; are just a few examples.

Trans-national Corporations (TNC)

The increase of neo-Colonialism mainly by the trans-national corporations whose massive monopoly of business and economy supported by selfish and unjust leadership have become a threat to the needed just and equal distribution of wealth and resources.

To this situation where 'Darker skinned' populations have become puppets of Western imperialism and are oppressing their own people, the Church in Africa has been playing the role of a prophetic voice, the champion of the oppressed and the voice of opposition in oppressive states.

It is not uncommon in many parts of Africa - to hear the Christian Church pointing to the evil of unjust distribution of property, downfall of morality, abuse of power and office through irresponsibility and undisciplined selfish conduct.

Pinkish Colored (White) Racism

In places where 'white' racism was the order of the day, the Church was seen as the champion of justice (caring for one's neighbor) as in the oppressive "insult" on Africans by Rhodesian Smith, and by the "cunning and diabolical" internal settlement and the Bantuization policy of the racist "apartheid" regime in South Africa.

In Uganda and elsewhere where persecution on the basis of ethnicity reflected yet another influence of European occupation in the minds and personalities of a few people in whose hands the leadership responsibility has accidently fallen. This alone presents the continent and the religious situation with a very challenging future.

Autocratic Rulers

Dictators in the name of one party systems, military regimes, or even multi-party systems, leave alone Marxist-Leninist ideology have occupied the African political scene. Pan-Africanism, the once goal to a political and social economic survival, has become only the voice of a concerned few in the current leadership of the Continent.

Role of All African Conference of Churches

The All African Conference of Churches, a Pan African organization, seems to have become the hope of the Church in Africa. This body has been fulfilling the role of African Church should occupy.

But it does its humanitarian and prophetic work under a strong pressure. Hopefully most people will expect it to live a life that challenges the socio-economic structures.

The A.A.C.C. with headquarters in Nairobi has a network of services in the whole continent, caring for Refugees, an increasingly big problem in the Continent where foreign inspired political upheavals have made people under persecution to cross their border to the next nation.

The role played by such an ecumenical body– A.A.C.C. as in the end of the 18 year Civil in Muslim led Sudan and the Christian South under the General Secretary of the body was crucial to the independence of South Sudan. .

8 RAPID URBANIZATION,SOCIAL CHANGE AND MORAL DECAY

Rapid Urbanization and Moral Decay

Increasing migrations to towns/cities, urbanization and the rapid growth spreading in African nations, is spreading the vices of corruption, bribery, and abuse of power let alone the downfall or breakdown of morality.

The rural areas are increasingly being isolated in the so-called developments policies or plans thus the old enemies of ignorance, disease and poverty are still challenges that the mission of the church is called to respond to, and meet.

"What is the use of skyscrapers in the big tourist and business cities, while the rural areas the majority or the masses are struggling as they have been doing even before the dawn of African independence?"

Every Sunday in the African scene, the churches are full of people, mostly women and including the youth, too. However, the majority of the Africans remain outside the Church and Christianity. These belong either to the traditional faith, Islam, or other of the world religions. These are the objective of Christian evangelization - and mission.

Churches as Resources

It is good to mention here that the Christian church has the resources to give hope, to liberate fully and to develop the African people. Just as it has the capacity to do the same to the whole of humanity. Its mission - therefore should address itself to the context of a people's existence their social, cultural, and ecological context.

In the African context this requires that the Western Churches to become aware of the changing trends. Africans are no longer what they used to be in the 18th century, neither are the Americans or the Europeans.

The world has become a small village if not a melting pot where the Negroid, the Caucasoid, and the Mongoloid come together in the name of humanity and dialogue together in the name of humanity.

We would also dialogue together concerning their future destiny (the world context). What is needed is international and intercultural missiology - a new sense of a both ecumenical and evangelical church in mission.

9 CONCLUSION

Missiological implication

If the Africans say that , we need to rethink about the implications of the mission of the church in their context; the Western churches should heed to their request.

They normally become defensive and complain, that the Africans and the rest of developing populations, cannot do without them. Moreover, after years of sacrifice in terms of personnel and resources in Africa or Asia and Latin America; these populations cannot just decide that they don't need Western missionaries.

Interdependence and Partnership

In a world of interdependence partnership requires each other, here, the westerners will find their mission in Africa and the Africans their mission in Europe or America.

The changing trends in the world requires better communication and interdependence among peoples of different places. Here lies the theology of the Christian mission or partnership in missionization.

We are all Ambassadors for Christ in mission to the Universe. Mission needs to be done everywhere , among your own people and across other peoples. We are the base and the field. (Not as it used to be Europe and North America - were the bases while the fields were Africa, Latin America, Asia, and the Oceania).

Africa is a part of the Universal Church of Christ, any missionary policy affecting their context or situation should be viewed from their point of view (not in a mission headquarters in Pasadena or London or Paris).

Liberation Theology of Mission

It is my feelings that the African context requires that theology of mission be exercised in the context of liberation.

Africans need to be liberated from external domination by western culture and exploitation and also the internal oppression by their selfish and exploitive leadership inspired by greed.

The contemporary political and economic situation in Africa, where the poor are getting more poor and the rich more richer is unacceptable in the context of freedom and justice.

While Africans are capable of their own leadership, some leaders are just opportunists and an extension of neo-colonialism and European imperialism occupation in land.

In the light of the Scriptures, the meaningful indigenous concepts of God, humans and nature should be applied to our condition if the people are going to be saved.

It is only after establishing our truly African identity and selfhood that we can contribute not only universally to the release of the souls of the masses from sin and wickedness but also help the poor and the oppressed by developing for them resources to attain their daily livelihood, human dignity, and the fullness thereof.

In conclusion may I borrow from other Africans:

... "there is a GOD in heaven' (Apolo Kivebulaya inspired by Acts 18:24) ..

. "GOD be thanked" (proclaimed Bishop Cyprian of Carthage as he was being beheaded) .

.. "though the greatest city of the world has fallen, the city of GOD abides forever (St. Augustine of Hippo) ..

. "It is no part of religion to compel religion which should be adopted freely, not by force" (St. Tertullian of Carthage).

10 REFERENCES

1. African Ecclesiastical Review; Volume 16, (1974) p. 427

2. Apter, David (1961). The Political Kingdom in Uganda: A Study of Bureaucratic Nationalism. Princeton University.

3. Baker, D. (ed.) (1972), "Heresy and Schism as Social and National Movements in Tanzania, Ill, DIA.", Studies in Church History, Vol. IX.

4. Barrett, and David B. (1968), Schism and Renewal in Africa, Nairobi: Oxford University Press.

5. Barnes, Timothy David (1984), "Tertullian the Antiquarian," Early Christianity and the Roman Empire. London: Variorum Reprints

6. Beason, E. W.(1897), Cyprian--His Life, His Time, His Work London: Longmans.

7. Beetham,T.A.,1967, Christianity and New Africa. New York; Frederick A. Prager.

8. Bray, L. (1980), Holiness and the Will of God: Perspectives on the Theology of Tertullian. John Knox Press.

9. Brown, Colin (1990). Christianity & Western Thought, Vol. 1. (Leicester: Apollos,), 91.

10. Chadwick, H (1967) The Early Church (London: Pelican Books, 1967): 116-121.

11. Cross, F.L. & Livingstone, eds. The Oxford Dictionary Of The Christian Church Oxford: OUP, 1990. p.920.

12. Cross, F.L. (1960)The Early Christian Fathers ,London: Oxford University Press.

13. Dickson, Kwesi, A. (1969), Biblical Revelation and African Beliefs, New York: Orbis.

14. Dodds, E.R, (1965), Pagan and Christian in an Age of Anxiety, London: Oxford University

15. Eliffe, V. (1969), Tanganyika Under Germany Rule, 1905, London, Cambridge University Press.

16. Encyclopedia Britannica, Yearbook,1977

17. Gatu, John (1972), "Call to Africanization," AACC Bulletin November Issue; Nairobi AACC

18. Idowu, E. Bolaji,(1968); African Tradition Religion,pp16-21. London.OUP.

19. New International Version. Bible. Book of Acts

20. Jacobs, Donald R., 1972, African Culture and African Church in A New. Look at Christianity in Africa, Vol. II No.2.p.5 Geneva: WSCF

21. Kaiser, Christopher B.(1991) Kaiser, Creation & The History of Science. London: Marshall Pickering.

22. Kenyatta, Jomo,(1965),Facing Mount Kenya; The Tribal life of the Gikuyu, NY; Random House/ Vintage

23. Kibicho, Samuel G.; (1970), Africa Traditional Religion and Christianity, in A New Look at Christianity in Africa, Vol. II No.2.p16 Geneva: W.S.C.F

24. Kihara, Nehemy N.(2016), Afrotheist Symbiosis; Christianity, Islam and Ethnic Religiosity in East Africa.,Bg.Publishing.

25. Kihara, Nehemy Ndirangu (1984). Religion and Politics in the Economic Development of Kenya and Tanzania, USA, D.A.I.

26. Lang, Andrew (1898), Making of Religion, London: Longmans Green Co.

27. Lindberg & Ronald L. Numbers, eds. (1986) God & Nature: Historical Essays on the Encounter Between Christianity and Science. Berkeley & Los Angeles: University of California Press, 26.

28. Luck, Anne (1963) African Saints: The, Story of Apolo Kivebulaya, London: SCM Press.

29. Mbiti, John;,(1969) African Religions and Philosophy., Nairobi; Heinemann

30. Norris, Richard A. (1966) God and World in Early Christian Theology: A Study in Justin Martyr, Irenaeus, Tertullian and Origen. London: Adam & Charles Black,), 86.

31. Oshitelu, G.A (2000)The African Fathers of the Early Church,Ibadan,U.o.,

32. P'Bitek, Okot (1970), African Religions in Western Scholarship, Nairobi: E.A.P.H.

33. Religious Information the World Almanac, `2016

34. Smith, Edman W. (1929) Aggrey of Africa: A Study in Black

and White. London: Student Christian Movement.

35. Stevenson, J.(1987)A New Eusebius: Documents Illustrating the History of the Church to AD 337. London: SPCK, 177.

36. Wiles, M.F.(1966) The Christian Fathers, London: Hodder and Stoughton,

37. World Almanac.,(2016); Information on Religious Affiliation.

ABOUT THE AUTHOR

The Revd. Prof. Dr. Nehemy Ndirangu Kihara was born in Nanyuki in Laikipia County of Kenya, East Africa.

He was educated at Timau in Meru County and Nairobi before graduating with a Licentiate of Theological Education from St. Paul's University (United Theological College), Limuru in Kiambu County.

He holds a Bachelor of Theology (B.Th.) in Biblical Literature and Geographic History from Christian International College.

He graduated with honors and attained a Master of Divinity (M.Div.) in Social Ethics, Psychology of Religion and Counseling, from the Interdenominational Theological Center at the Clark Atlanta University Complex.

He also attained a Doctor of Philosophy (Ph.D.) in Anthropology, Sociology of Religion and Political Science from Emory University.

As an Investigative Journalist and Radio Broadcaster this Independent Publisher hosted a weekend English and still hosts a weekly Swahili Community Show for Sagal Radio Services at WATB 1420 AM Station in Decatur, GA.

As an Interdisplinary Educator he taught Security Management and Police Studies for the Institute of Peace and Security Studies, (now known as the Department of Security and Correctional Science) of Kenyatta University in Nanyuki Campus, where he was the Coordinator of Humanities and Examinations Officer.

The Author also taught Introductory Psychology, Sociology, Criminal Procedure and Law of Evidence, Intelligence-Led Policing, Public Administration and General Management Principles among other units at the Nyeri and Embu Campuses.

He was an Adjunct Professor of Sociology/ Social Sciences at the Atlanta Campus of Saint Leo University, Tampa, Fl. Taught such courses as Anthropology, Sociology, and Criminal Justice units as Social Theory, Drugs and Society, Marriage and Family, Research Methods, Human Behavior, among others He was an Adjunct Professor of Ethics at the Georgia Campus (Henry Medical Center) of the College of Health, University of St. Francis, Joliet, Ill.,

The Author was also the founding Moderating Bishop of the Ujamaa Nomadic Church -Without Borders, as a new church-mission initiative in US. He had also been an Urban Renewal/ Organizing Pastor of Beth Salem United Presbyterian Church, Columbus, Georgia. He served as an International Missionary in California, Iowa and New York, under the Mission to US program of the Presbyterian Church, USA

As a Senior Lecturer at Kenyatta University, the Author taught African Culture, Belief Systems, Social Theory and Research Methods units in the Department of Philosophy and Religious Studies and also in the Department of Sociology. He was also an Activist Educator, who fought for academic freedom and excellence, which led to his unfair dismissal by the government which controlled the public universities and educational institutions.

Reverend Professor Ndirangu Kihara started his career a high school teacher and principal at Muthithi Secondary School, and then an ordained Church Minister of Muthithi Parish and the Stated Clerk of the wider Murang'a Presbytery of the Presbyterian Church of East Africa.

NEHEMY N. KIHARA

BLUERGREEN PUBLISHERS